ADVENT IS A TI
TO WAIT FOR JESUS

During Advent we count the weeks until Christmas. The candles of the Advent wreath remind us to wait for Jesus and to prepare a place for him in our hearts. We light one candle on each of the four Sundays of Advent. Their bright flames bring light to our lives and hope into our world.

ACTIVITY → *Color three of the candles purple and one of them pink. Then color one of the flames. You will come back to this page each Sunday in Advent to color the rest of the flames. Add decorations that remind you of Jesus' love for you.*

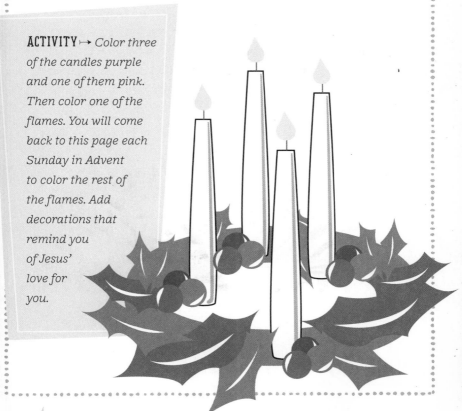

Jesus, help me to make this Advent a time to prepare my heart for your coming.

1

ADAM AND EVE

In the Bible we read the story about the first people God created—a man named Adam and a woman named Eve. God breathed life into them and gave them a home in a beautiful garden.

This story reminds us of how Jesus wants us to be happy and to share with others. By caring for the gifts of God's creation, we make the world a happier place!

ACTIVITY ↪ *Fill in the picture of the garden by drawing plants, trees, flowers, and animals. Color your picture and share it with your family.*

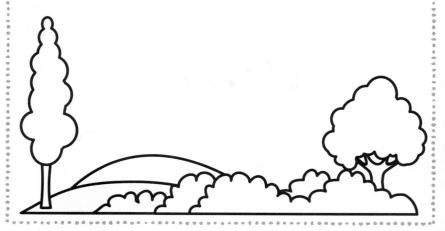

Jesus, show me how to take care of the gifts of God's creation.

ADVENT IS A TIME OF LOVE

Jesus taught us to love God and to love one another. We call this the Great Commandment. During Advent, we can show our love for God and others by being kind and thoughtful. We can practice forgiveness and help the people in our families.

ACTIVITY ↦ *A word web is a way to connect one word to another. Fill in the web with words that connect to love. One of these is done for you.*

SHARE

LOVE

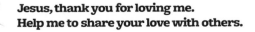

Jesus, thank you for loving me.
Help me to share your love with others.

NOAH AND THE ARK

The Bible tells how the people turned against God
and did terrible things to one another. God decided to make
a new beginning by sending a flood to cover the earth.
Noah was a good man. God told him to build an ark and to
take his family and two of every kind of animal, bird,
and insect on the boat to escape the flood. After the flood Noah
sent a bird in search of land. He gave thanks to God for saving
him and his family.

When Jesus came to us, it was also a new beginning. Advent
is a time to thank God for giving us the gift of Jesus.

ACTIVITY →
*Draw a line
between the
two animals
that belong
together.*

**Jesus, show me how to take care of
the gifts of God's creation.**

4

PRAYING WITH THE PSALMS

The psalms are prayers of love and praise.
We pray or sing a psalm each time we go to Mass.
During Advent, the psalms express our joy and help us
to open our hearts to Jesus.

ACTIVITY ↦ *Use the code to complete the words of the psalm.*

C	D	E	F	G	H	I	J	L	M	N	O	R	S	T	U	Y
1	2	3	4	5	6	7	8	9	10	11	12	13	14	15	16	17

$$\overline{1}\ \overline{12}\ \overline{10}\ \overline{3,}\qquad \overline{9}\ \overline{3}\ \overline{15}$$

$$\overline{16}\ \overline{14}\qquad \overline{14}\ \overline{7}\ \overline{11}\ \overline{5}$$

$$\overline{8}\ \overline{12}\ \overline{17}\ \overline{4}\ \overline{16}\ \overline{9}\ \overline{9}\ \overline{17}$$

$$\overline{15}\ \overline{12}\qquad \overline{15}\ \overline{6}\ \overline{3}$$

$$\overline{9}\ \overline{12}\ \overline{13}\ \overline{2.}$$

PSALM 95:1

**Jesus, help me to celebrate Advent
by praying each day.**

GETTING READY FOR CHRISTMAS

Advent is a time to prepare our hearts for Christmas. We do fun things with our families and friends. The holidays are a happy time in our homes, neighborhoods, schools, and parishes. This is a special time to welcome Jesus into our hearts.

ACTIVITY → *Use the picture clues to fill in the crossword puzzle.*

Down

Across

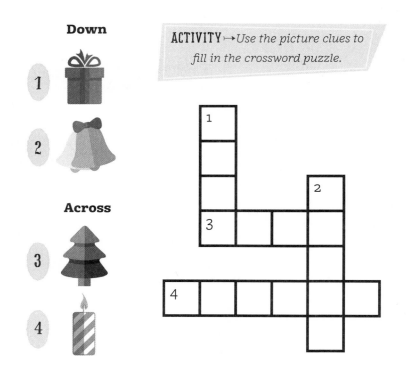

Jesus, I am excited for Christmas. Help me to make this Advent a time of joy as I welcome you into my heart.

ABRAHAM AND SARAH

Abraham and Sarah waited many years to have a child. They trusted God when he told them to move to a new land. God promised that they would have a family and that their children's children would be as numerous as the stars in the sky. They were filled with joy.

Jesus reminds us that God always keeps his promises. Next time you look at the stars, remember the promise God made to Abraham and Sarah.

ACTIVITY → *Connect the small stars to find the great promise of love God gave us.*

Jesus, help me to trust in you and to remember your love for me.

ADVENT IS A TIME TO GIVE THANKS

One way we prepare to welcome Jesus during Advent is by praying each day. One of the most important ways to pray is by giving thanks. We thank God for the people in our lives, for the good things we enjoy, and for the gift of our lives.

This is the Second Sunday of Advent. Go back to the first Sunday and color another flame on the Advent wreath.

ACTIVITY⟶*Make a list of people and things you are thankful for. Then write a prayer of thanksgiving.*

Jesus, thank you for coming into the world and for teaching us about God's love and mercy.

JACOB'S DREAM

Jacob was the grandson of Abraham and Sarah. One day, he fought with his brother and ran into the desert to hide. He was scared and missed his family. That night he fell asleep and had a dream. He saw a ladder reaching to the sky with angels going up and down. In the dream God told him not to be afraid. Jacob awoke and knew that God was with him in that place.

ACTIVITY →
Fill in the missing letters on the ladder to read about Jesus' dream for our lives.

LO_E

_NE

A_OTH_R

Jesus, when I feel scared and lonely, help me to remember that you are always with me.

ADVENT IS A TIME TO SHARE

During Advent we remember people who are in need. Many parishes prepare gifts for children who won't have much this Christmas. Talk to your family about something you can do to help people in need during Advent.

> **ACTIVITY** → *Fill the stocking with gifts for a child in need.*

 Jesus, bless all children of the world, especially those without homes to live in and food to eat.

JOSEPH AND HIS COAT OF MANY COLORS

Jacob had twelve sons. He loved them all, but his son Joseph held a special place in his heart. He made Joseph a coat of many colors. Joseph's brothers grew jealous. One day they took away his coat and sold him to strangers. Joseph was taken to a faraway land where he became an advisor to the king. Many years later, his brothers came to ask the king for help. When Joseph saw them, he forgave them for what they had done to him.

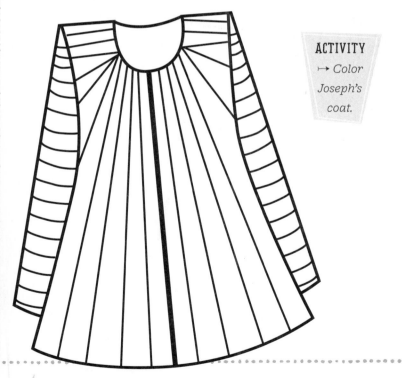

ACTIVITY
↪ Color Joseph's coat.

Jesus, help me to be forgiving and to ask for forgiveness when I hurt others.

LOOKING FOR SIGNS OF GOD'S GOODNESS

Jesus taught his followers to use their eyes
and ears to look and listen for how God is present in our world.
Each day we can watch for ways in which God's love and
beauty are present in the people and places around us.

ACTIVITY → *Draw a circle around something
that is different in each Christmas tree.*

 **Jesus, the world is filled with signs of your goodness
and love. Help me to watch for them today.**

MOSES LEADS GOD'S PEOPLE TO SAFETY

FRIDAY
December 9

*Second Week
in Advent*

Moses was a good and faithful man. One day, God called him to take the people out of the land of Egypt, where they lived as slaves, and take them to a new land. Even though he was afraid, Moses did as God asked. He led the people across the wilderness to the land God promised.

ACTIVITY →

Help Moses find a way to the land God promised to the people.

THE PROMISED LAND

Jesus, help me to follow you by obeying your law of love.

13

ADVENT IS A SEASON TO SHARE OUR LOVE

We are halfway through Advent! There are just two weeks until we celebrate Christmas. This is a time to remember to share our love by praying to God, forgiving each other, and sharing with those in need. How are you making Advent a time to prepare for Jesus?

> **ACTIVITY** ↦ *Find these words in the puzzle and circle them going up, down, or across.*

PRAY ★ FORGIVE ★ SHARE

W	P	P	G	X	T	C	V	N
F	O	R	G	I	V	E	G	E
A	Q	A	B	Y	F	L	P	R
O	L	Y	H	T	E	I	D	A
P	K	B	E	S	W	F	C	H
L	V	U	G	H	T	E	R	S

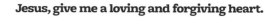

Jesus, give me a loving and forgiving heart.

CELEBRATING ADVENT WITH OUR FAMILIES

Advent is a special time to be with our families.
We prepare holiday meals and share traditions. We go to Mass
and pray for others. We look for ways to help each other and to
be kind, loving, considerate, and generous. What are you doing
to help your family welcome Jesus into your hearts this Advent?

This is the Third Sunday of Advent. Go back to the first
Sunday and color another flame on the Advent wreath.

ACTIVITY ↦ *Circle the traditions that happen during Advent.*
Cross out those that don't.

DECORATE THE TREE

CARVE A PUMPKIN

COLOR EGGS

SING CAROLS

WRAP GIFTS

SET OFF FIREWORKS

Jesus, thank you for my family. Open our hearts to your love.

15

RUTH AND NAOMI HELPED EACH OTHER

Naomi had two sons. One of them married a woman named Ruth. The family was very happy. Then Naomi's husband and sons died. Naomi wanted Ruth to return to her own family so she wouldn't suffer. Ruth wanted to stay with Naomi so they could help one another. The two women worked together to find food. Ruth met a kind man named Boaz. Boaz married Ruth and provided a home for Naomi.

Ruth and Naomi remind us of how important it is to trust in God's love and to help each other.

ACTIVITY → *Write a list of ways to be a good friend.*

_____

_____

_____

_____

_____

_____

Jesus, show me how to be a good and loyal friend.

JESUS TEACHES US HOW TO FORGIVE

Jesus told a story about a boy who took his father's money and ran away from home. After spending it, he had nothing to eat. He was afraid and missed his family. He felt bad about thinking only of himself. When he returned home, his father greeted him with great joy and forgave him for being so selfish. Jesus told the story to show how God is always ready to forgive us.

ACTIVITY ⇢ *Use the key to find something else Jesus taught about forgiveness.*

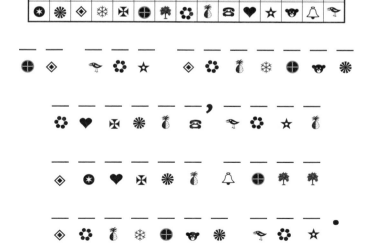

Jesus, help me to forgive those who hurt me. Remind me to ask for forgiveness when I hurt someone else.

SAMUEL LISTENED TO GOD'S VOICE

Samuel was a boy who lived with a holy man named Eli. One night Samuel heard a voice calling his name. He ran to Eli, but Eli said he did not call him. Samuel heard the voice a second time and ran to Eli. Eli told him the same thing and sent him back to bed. A third time, Samuel heard the voice and ran to Eli. This time Eli understood that God was calling Samuel. He told Samuel to listen to God's voice and to do as God commanded.

ACTIVITY ↦
Circle the words that describe a person who listens for God's voice.

PRAYERFUL

LOVING

MEAN

ANGRY

PEACEFUL

WORRIED

JOYFUL

Jesus, be with me when I pray so that I can listen for what you want me to say and do.

PRAYERS OF BLESSING

A blessing is a prayer in which we dedicate someone or something to God. When we say a prayer of blessing before meals, we offer our food and ourselves to God. During Advent there are many chances to offer prayers of blessing. We can bless the tree after we decorate it, the gifts we wrap, and the food we share. Each time, we are reminded of the goodness of God.

ACTIVITY ↦ *Complete the words of this blessing by filling in your own words. Share your blessing with your family.*

Loving God, bless our

_____ •

Help us to

_____ •

Thank you for

_____ •

Jesus, bless our home and all the people who share our Advent joy.

THE HOLY FAMILY

Jesus had a family who loved him. Together they shared meals and helped one another. Mary and Joseph took care of Jesus and taught him how to pray. They told him stories and gave him chores to do.

Like Jesus, it is important to respect our parents and other adults who take care of us.

> **ACTIVITY** ↪ *Draw a picture of your family doing something to celebrate Advent.*

 Jesus, watch over my family and all families. Show us how to love and respect each other.

KING DAVID LOVED MUSIC

David was chosen by God to be king of Israel. David loved music. He played the harp and wrote songs. Sometimes he was so joyful over God's love that he danced.

Singing carols is a favorite way to celebrate Christmas. We express our love and joy because Jesus is coming into our hearts in a new way.

ACTIVITY ↦ *Use the words below to complete this famous Christmas carol.*

CALM

Silent _ _ _ _ _.

BRIGHT

_ _ _ _ night.

NIGHT

All is _ _ _ _.

HOLY

All is _ _ _ _ _ _ .

Jesus, I am so happy that you are coming into my heart. Help me to prepare a place for you.

JOHN THE BAPTIST PREPARED FOR JESUS' COMING

John the Baptist was a prophet who told people to prepare for Jesus by changing the way they lived. When we make loving choices, we show our love for Jesus.

This is the Fourth Sunday of Advent. Go back to the first Sunday and color the last flame on the Advent wreath.

> **ACTIVITY** → *Show how you can change a poor choice into a loving one by filling in the blanks.*

Instead of fighting, I can

_____ •

Instead of saying something mean, I can

_____ •

Instead of complaining, I can

_____ •

 Jesus, remind me to make choices that show my love for you.

22

SOLOMON WAS A WISE KING 🍃

After David died, his son Solomon became king. Solomon was a wise man who helped people make good choices. When we follow Jesus, we make choices that are good for us and that show love for others.

ACTIVITY →
Use the chart to color King Solomon's crown.

❶=yellow ❹=green

❷=red ❺=orange

❸=blue ❻=purple

Jesus, help me to make choices that show my love for you.

23

ADVENT IS A TIME TO OPEN OUR HEARTS

All during Advent, we have been preparing our hearts to welcome Jesus. We do this through the loving words and actions we share with others and by being respectful, kind, generous, and considerate. How has your heart grown more loving this Advent?

ACTIVITY ⟶ *Complete the drawing of the heart. In the center, write or draw how you are opening your heart to Jesus.*

Jesus, open my heart to your love so that I can share that same love with others.

JOSEPH CARED FOR JESUS

Joseph was a carpenter and the husband of Mary. When God asked him to care for Mary and Jesus, Joseph obeyed. He kept his family safe and shared his love with them.

Our parents care for us in the same way Joseph did for his family. During Advent we can show our parents that we are grateful for their love.

ACTIVITY →
Circle the tools that a carpenter would use, and cross out the ones that don't belong.

Jesus, thank you for all those who keep me safe and teach me about your love.

GIVING THE GIFT OF LOVE

One way we celebrate Christmas is by giving each other presents. The best gifts are those that come from the heart. When we are thankful, forgiving, kind, and generous, we give others the gift of love.

ACTIVITY → *Fill each present with a gift of love. Choose a word from the list below to place in one of the packages.*

thanks ★ peace worry ★ anger ★ joy

Jesus, open my heart to your love so that I can share that same love with others.

MARY IS THE MOTHER OF JESUS

FRIDAY
December 23

Fourth Week in Advent

Mary was a young girl who gave her heart to God.
One day, an angel appeared to her and told her she was
to be the mother of Jesus. Mary said yes to God. She responded
with a prayer of great joy.

ACTIVITY ↪ *Use the code to fill in Mary's prayer of joy.*

A	C	D	E	F	G	H	I	L	M	N	O	P	R	S	T	U	Y
1	2	3	4	5	6	7	8	9	10	11	12	13	14	15	16	17	18

___ ___   ___ ___ ___ ___
10 18   15 12 17 9

___ ___ ___ ___ ___ ___ ___ ___
13 14 12 2 9 1 8 10 15

___ ___ ___   ___ ___ ___ ___ ___ ___ ___ ___
16 7 4   6 14 4 1 16 11 4 15 15

___ ___   ___ ___ ___   ___ ___ ___ ___ •
12 5   16 7 4   9 12 14 3

Jesus, help me to be like your mother, Mary, by following you and sharing your love.

CHRISTMAS IS ALMOST HERE!

We are reaching the end of Advent. During this holy season we have learned about the ancestors of Jesus who followed the way of God. How have you opened your heart this Advent in order to listen to God and to follow the way of Jesus?

> **ACTIVITY** → *Match each ancestor of Jesus with the words that describe him or her.*

MOSES — I stayed loyal to Naomi and helped her

MARY — I was a king who loved music

DAVID — I had a coat of many colors

JOSEPH — I led the people to the land God promised

RUTH — I said yes to God and am the mother of Jesus

Jesus, thank you for all of the people who show me how to follow you.